MUSIC MINUS ONE
BEGINNING
CONTEST SOLOS

CD
3911

CASS.
8051

LAUREATE SERIES

Meditation

GIUSEPPE CONCONE
Trans. by William Gower

Andante con moto

Nocturno

from "Midsummer Night's Dream"

FELIX MENDELSSOHN
Trans. by George J. Trinkaus

Andante tranquillo

Camping Out

LEONARD B. SMITH
Edited by Leonard V. Falcone

Andante moderato

Saraband

G. F. HANDEL
Trans. by William Gower

Largo

Romance

ANTON RUBINSTEIN, Op. 44, No. 1
Arr. by Leonard B. Smith
Edited by Leonard V. Falcone

Moderato

Ballad

PAUL TANNER

Andante

Autumn Soliloquy

CARL FRANGKISER

Andante moderato

Apollo

FORREST L. BUCHTEL

Andante

COMPACT DISC PAGE AND BAND INFORMATION

Music Minus One

MMO CD 3911
MMO Cass. 8051

LAUREATE SERIES CONTEST SOLOS
BEGINNING LEVEL FOR TROMBONE, VOL. 1

LAUREATE SERIES

TROMBONE MUSIC

TUNING
Before the piano accompaniment begins you will hear four tuning notes, followed by a short scale and another tuning note. This will enable you to tune your instrument to the record.

4

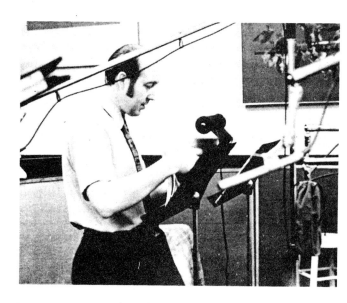

PERFORMANCE GUIDE
COMMENTARY BY PER BREVIG

CONCONE
Meditation

The eighth notes in the piano accompaniment will help decide the tempo of Concone's "Meditation." If it is too slow, it will be tiring. This is a good piece for practicing attacks. Every note must be supported from the diaphragm; there must be no percussive tongue snap. Play with a good, full sound. Although the piece is marked *piano,* you must not play so softly that you lose control. Because it is so sustained, it would be helpful to think of how a cellist would play it. Your air column must be like the cellist's bow. When you breathe, take care not to disturb the musical line. Even though the breath must be taken quickly, it must also be very deep. Really open up!

MENDELSSOHN

Nocturno from *Midsummer Night's Dream*

This piece in G Major will give good practice in playing the D in fourth position. Remember when you tune, the D is a little sharp on most instruments, so you will probably have to compensate by pulling the slide out slightly. Listen very carefully and don't move the slide too much; it must be only a little. You might practice a G in fourth position, then a B — pull the slide in slightly. Then play a D in fourth position, and pull the slide out a little. (This works on most instruments, but not all.)

The two fermatas sometimes found in this music are not necessary. They have the effect of simply stretching the two quarter notes, and have no real musical value. (It is doubtful if Mendelssohn had them in the original edition.) This piece demands many quick breaths. If you feel that the music wants to move forward, especially in the middle section, go with it! Let the music move and flow, but never run. There may be a slight broadening on the two quarter notes just before the restatement of the opening theme, in measure 26, and then the theme may be played a little slower than the beginning. The ritard at the end is obvious.

SMITH

Camping Out

This Andante moderato is perhaps slightly faster than you would imagine. It is like a march, not too fast, with a *maestoso* feeling. The phrases are long, extending four bars, so it is a good idea to breathe after the third

beat of the second (solo) measure. The last beat then becomes a pick-up to the next bar.

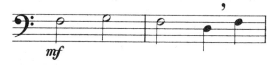

This pattern continues through the entire piece. The quarter note pick-ups should be rather sustained, with a nice attack, but not too legato.

Although the Poco allegretto section is marked staccato, it should not be too short. Each attack must have support from the diaphragm. Don't use a sharp, hard tongue. Notes should not sound percussive, as if you were hitting them. Play each note detached, but with deep, full support.

Notice the little ritard in measure 31. The accents should not be too heavy; let them have a little lift. Pay attention to the dynamics, and get the contrast between mf and p.

Notice the little ritard in measure 31. The accents should not be too heavy; let them have a little lift. Pay attention to the dynamics, and get the contrast between *mf* and *p.*

HANDEL
Saraband

This Saraband is from the F Minor Concerto. When it was transcribed for trombone, it was transposed into a lower key, and the ornaments were removed. This piece is very difficult at a slow tempo. Keep the tempo steady, but don't drag. Remember, if you are uncomfortable, the audience will be restless.

Every time you have skips which may be difficult, such as in the third measure, make a slight crescendo up to the high note.

It is better to "lean into it" than to hold back and miss the note! The same advice applies to measure 7, in the interval from F up to E flat. Go after the E flat and you will get it!

In the beginning, play a good, full mf; then at the repeat in measure 10, try to get a feeling of p, but don't try to play too soft. A *piano* passage must not be forced or strained.

Another possibility would be to let the accompanist take the repeat (at bar 10) alone. The trombone could re-enter at bar 19, and would be fresh to go on up into the slightly higher register. When you get to measure 19 the music must go forward. Don't hold back.

The breath marks, for the most part, define phrases. You may even have to sneak a breath in between. Take the breath very fast, and don't break the musical line. When ever you breathe, go all the way down to the diaphragm. Fill up! Don't just breathe with the mouth and nose.

RUBINSTEIN
Romance

Because the Rubinstein "Romance" is such a song-type piece, the student might try to sing a few bars, and then play the way he sang. This approach often works very well. Playing a wind instrument is very much like singing. If the student will listen to fine singers, and sing himself sometimes, the style of the music will often be better understood.

The trombone entrance should be played portamento — not staccato and not a regular slur. It must be tongued, but very sustained. Allow the music to move forward. Play with it, and use a full, smooth tone.

TANNER
Ballad

Paul Tanner is a trombonist in California, and his Ballad is a very sustained, legato piece. There are many long phrases, and of course you have to breathe between them. You must practice breathing as quickly as possible, so that you don't split the phrases. Take a breath after the E-natural in measure 6.

This is the kind of breathing this piece demands. The first phrase extends over four bars, and most people will not be able to play it in one breath. The best place to sneak a breath is after a tied note. But remember, there must not be any noticeable holes in the music. At measure 21, the piece will benefit from a *piu mosso*. It is much more interesting when it moves forward. The pianist should ritard before measure 33. When the ritard is made, it should return to the original tempo, never slower.

FRANGKISER
Autumn Soliloquy

The composer put much expressive, melancholic music into this piece. He has indicated, with all sorts of crescendos, decrescendos, legatos, etc., just exactly how it should go. The most important thing to do with this piece is to express, with little nuances here and there. Sometimes you may taper off, or slightly ritard a phrase, but when you begin the next phrase, you must be sure you are back in tempo. Do not let it drag.

In the 13th bar, a slight accelerando might be in order. Let the music move forward. You can make it more intense by increasing the vibrato as you crescendo. It won't become frantic, but it will have more feeling. There is no consistent rule for using vibrato. Whenever music sounds better with it, by all means use it. Vibrato is not an essential ingredient of trombone sound. It does not have the same importance for a trombonist that it has for a flutist, for example. It is not always used in orchestral playing, but some solos do benefit from it.

BUCHTEL
Apollo

This is a "fun" piece which offers us many opportunities to practice. It is marked Andante, and shouldn't be too fast. Don't make the sixteenth notes too short. They must have correct value. Notice the marking at 13, "slightly faster." Give a little added vigor there, and then go back to your original tempo. Follow the markings in the music.

At 45, "smoothly," play very sustained and lyrically for contrast. Tongue it, but keep the legato character. When the main theme returns, play light and easy. Don't overblow the *forte* parts; the tone must not get brassy.

When you play in the key of E flat, you should play the D in fourth position. If you are playing a fast B, C, D, do not play 1, 2, 1. Positions 1, 2, 4 will give a much more natural movement to the slide.

Do not call this a "false" position. It is an alternate position. Always remember, the slide should move back and forth as naturally as possible.

MEDITATION

Side B - Band 1 ♩ = 88 (2'00")

GIUSEPPE CONCONE
Trans. by William Gower

8051

NOCTURNO
from "Midsummer Night's Dream"

Side B - Band 2 ♩ = 66 (1'45")

FELIX MENDELSSOHN
Trans. by George J. Trinkaus

5 beats precede music

Andante tranquillo

8051

CAMPING OUT

LEONARD B. SMITH
Edited by Leonard V. Falcone

Side B - Band 3 (2'40")

8051

SARABAND

Side B - Band 4   ♩ = 66 (2'06")

G. F. HANDEL
Trans. by William Gower

3 beats precede music

8051

ROMANCE

Side B - Band 5 ♩ = 80 (2'00")

ANTON RUBINSTEIN, Op. 44, No. 1
Arr. by Leonard B. Smith
Edited by Leonard V. Falcone

8051

Y. 11746

BALLAD

Side B - Band 6 ♩ = 84 (1'57")

PAUL TANNER

8051

AUTUMN SOLILOQUY

Side B - Band 7   ♩ = 92 (2'41")

CARL FRANGKISER

8051

APOLLO

Side B - Band 8 (3'13")
Side B - Band 9 (3'34")

FORREST L. BUCHTEL

8051

S LAUREATE SERIES

MMO MUSIC GROUP, INC., 50 Executive Boulevard, Elmsford, NY 10523-1325